Copyright © 2022 Matthew Douglas Pinard

All Rights Reserved. No part of this book publication may be reproduced or transmitted in any form or by any means, mechanical or electronic, including photocopying, scanning, and recording, or by any information storage and retrieval system, or other -- without prior permission in writing from the author or publisher. Disclaimers: The Publisher and the Author make no representation or warranties concerning the accuracy or completeness of the contents of this work and specifically disclaim all warranties for a particular purpose. No warranty may be created or extended through sales or promotional materials. The advice and strategies contained herein may not be suitable for every situation. This work is sold with the understanding that the Author and Publisher are not engaged in rendering legal, technological, or other professional services. If professional assistance is required, the services of a competent professional should be sought. Neither the Publisher nor the Author shall be liable for damages arising therefrom. The fact that an organization or website is referred to in this work as a citation and/or potential source of further information does not mean that the Author or the Publisher endorses the information, the organization, or website it may provide, or recommendations it may make. Further, readers should be aware that the websites listed in this work may have changed or disappeared between the time that this work was written and when it is read. Details of the cases and stories in this book have been changed to preserve privacy.

Printed in the United States of America
Published by:
Writer's Publishing House
Prescott, Az 86301

Cover and Interior Design by Creative Artistic Excellence Marketing
Project Management and Book Launch by Creative Artistic Excellence Marketing
https://lizzymcnett.com

Paperback ISBN: 978-1-64873-245-4
Hardcover ISBN: 978-1-64873-246-1
Ebook ISBN: 978-1-64873-247-8

TABLE OF CONTENTS

"The Lion's Gate" 6

"Venus Trine Mars" 46

G is for Greg 85

A Shower of Roses 90

J is for Jeff 99

K is for Kristy 104

The Qui Tam Case and A Canary 114

Apocalypse Now 121

Twin Queens 130

Addendum 146

Other Books by Author Matthew Douglas Pinard 147

Screenplay Awards 147

Matthew Douglas Pinard 147

The Lion's Gate

CHAPTER ONE:
"The Lion's Gate"

The Lion's Gate opening on August 8th, 2021 was an event unlike any I can recall in my four and a half decades of this life. Not only has this incredible portal opened up from Eden to Earth, but the signs and wonders since this event have been equally impressive.

The spiritual alignment has been celebrated for centuries. Civilizations as far back as the Dogon tribe of Africa, Sumer, and Ancient Egypt tracked Sirius across the sky. Sirius' rising and alignment with the sun was considered a significant event in many ancient cultures.

As beautiful and unmistakably angelic as these signs have been, they are accompanied by unimaginable displays of true king authority on Earth. For example, a recent earthquake on September 7th, 2021 in Mexico struck 7.0 on the Richter scale. An odd blue-shaped light in the form of a cross appeared above the city simultaneously, leaving many locals to describe the event as an "apocalypse." It was one display of the power of God from 2021.

Sirius' position on Earth coincides with the Orion constellation aligning perfectly with the pyramids of Giza, thereby creating a trinity of alignments that open the Lion's Gate portal. In my previous books, I asserted that we are descendants of an alien race called the Anunnaki, who built the pyramids.

Since the event took place in 2021 during the super moons, the date brings forth a spiritual window of new opportunities for abundant new beginnings.

Another 6.9 magnitude earthquake struck the Alaskan island chain on October 11th, 2021, and a 6.4 magnitude earthquake struck Greece on October 12th, 2021. Other incredible events included the fiftieth eruption of Mt. Etna in Italy in less than one year.

2021 saw multiple volcanoes on the Aleutian Alaskan chain of islands occur simultaneously. We have seen other eruptions in Iceland at the Fagradalsfjall volcano, and more volcanic activity at Hawaii's Kilauea. Each day has witnessed an earthquake of 4.0 to 8.0 on the Richter scale.

In 2021, we witnessed heat waves in the Pacific Northwest that broke all standing temperature records and left hundreds dead from heatstroke. In my new home state of Arizona, the reservoir system that we rely on for water at Lake Mead dropped to its lowest level in recorded history. Scientists stated this heatwave could have only been the result of mankind's imprint on the environment.

We also witnessed massive flooding in the central United States, which claimed dozens of lives. Recent headlines read that "in California droughts and wildfires are the 'new normal" as wildfires reached higher and higher altitudes in that state. Wildfires also spread across Greece and Hawaii, killing hundreds.

The 2020 to 2021 hurricane seasons have been the most active on record. In 2020, 11 named storms hit landfall, and already 8 named storms with landfall in 2021.

Louisiana saw two category 4 hurricanes, Laura and Ida. Hurricane Ida was the strongest storm since Katrina. All of these events have surrounded a continuing global pandemic, with a new Delta variant that has continued to claim many lives. Whether to vaccinate has become a hotly contested issue that has divided not only families (my wife is anti-Vax, while I have been forced to get the vaccine to keep my job as a retinal surgical sales representative), but we have seen this become a major political football, with some medical professionals outwardly disagreeing on a multitude of levels.

In a recent television interview a critical care nurse was told she would lose her job by refusing vaccination. She went on to state she saw unusual heart conditions and strokes among those vaccinated who ended, up contracting COVID-19 anyway.

Despite all the tragic uncertainties, I witnessed truly beautiful displays of other kingdom power and glory in the form of more incredible angel photos.

As a Son of God, I am here to simply bear witness, praying this fallen world changes, or face going down the ship. I maintain hope that somehow the world will wake up to certain realities. We cannot sustain the current course of action without massive destruction, which could make life on this planet very difficult.

A celestial event like the opening of the Lion's Gate Portal is considered one of the luckiest days of the year. The portal is a combination of our sun being in its home sign of Leo, Sirius rising in the skies, and the numerical number of 8/8/2021.

Photo: An amazing image of the Lion's Gate portal opening above Prescott Valley, Arizona on August 8th, 2021. I see two huge sunlit angel wings opening the portal.

Three days prior to the opening of the Lion's Gate on August 8th, 2021 I received numerous angelic signs and wonders in the skies above Prescott Valley, Arizona. On August 5th, 2021 all of these amazing images appeared above our neighborhood.

Photo: An amazing image of the Lion's Gate portal opening above Prescott Valley, Arizona on August 8th, 2021. This close up of angels opening the portal is simply beautiful.

Photo: On August 5th, 2021 this incredible face appeared above our home in Prescott Valley, Arizona.

Photo: On August 5th, 2021 this incredible angel sylph wing appeared directly above our home in Prescott Valley, Arizona.

Photo: On August 5th, 2021 this incredible angel sylph wing appeared directly above our home in Prescott Valley, Arizona.

Photo: On August 5th, 2021 this incredible angel sylph wing appeared directly above our home in Prescott Valley, Arizona.

Photo: On August 5th, 2021 this incredible angel sylph wing appeared directly above our home in Prescott Valley, Arizona.

Photo: On August 5th, 2021 this incredible angel sylph wing appeared directly above our home in Prescott Valley, Arizona.

Photo: On August 5th, 2021 this incredible angel sylph wing appeared directly above our home in Prescott Valley, Arizona.

Photo: On August 5th, 2021 this incredible angel sylph wing appeared directly above our home in Prescott Valley, Arizona.

Photo: On August 5th, 2021 this incredible angel sylph wing appeared directly above our home in Prescott Valley, Arizona.

Photo: On August 5th, 2021 this incredible angel sylph wing appeared directly above our home in Prescott Valley, Arizona.

Photo: On August 5th, 2021 this incredible angel sylph wing appeared directly above our home in Prescott Valley, Arizona.

Photo: On August 6th, 2021 this incredible angel sylph wing appeared directly above our home in Prescott Valley, Arizona. This was two days before the Lion's Gate opening.

Photo: On August 9th, 2021 this incredible angel sylph wing and face appeared directly above our home in Prescott Valley, Arizona.

Photo: On August 9th, 2021 this incredible angel sylph wing and face appeared directly above our home in Prescott Valley, Arizona.

Photo: On August 9th, 2021 this incredible pair of angel sylphs facing off like in a deep conversation appeared directly above our home in Prescott Valley, Arizona.

Photo: On August 9th, 2021 this incredible angel sylph wing and face appeared directly above our home in Prescott Valley, Arizona. You can see a head near the top middle and a wing pointing the way.

Photo: On August 9th, 2021 this incredible angel sylph wing and face appeared directly above Prescott, Arizona.

Photo: On August 9th, 2021 this incredible angel sylph wing and faced sunset appeared directly above our home in Prescott Valley, Arizona.

Photo: On August 9th, 2021 this incredible angel sylph wing and faced sunset appeared directly above our home in Prescott Valley, Arizona.

Photo: On August 9th, 2021 this incredible angel sylph wing and faced sunset appeared directly above our home in Prescott Valley, Arizona.

Photo: On August 9th, 2021 this incredible angel sylph wing and faced sunset appeared directly above our home in Prescott Valley, Arizona.

Photo: On August 9th, 2021 this incredible angel sylph wing and double face appeared directly above our home in Prescott Valley, Arizona. You can clearly see a human like face staring to the right with a huge nose.

Photo: On August 10th, 2021 this incredible angel sylph wing and faced sunset appeared directly above our home in Prescott Valley, Arizona.

Photo: On August 10th, 2021 this incredible angel sylph wing appeared directly above our home in Prescott Valley, Arizona.

Photo: On August 10th, 2021 this incredible angel sylph wing appeared directly above our home in Prescott Valley, Arizona.

Photo: On August 10th, 2021 this incredible angel sylph wing appeared directly above our home in Prescott Valley, Arizona.

Photo: On August 10th, 2021 this incredible angel sylph wing appeared directly above the Garden of Stone at St. Germaine Catholic Church in Prescott Valley, Arizona. As I mentioned in my book "Kingdom Come" I believe The Garden of Stone to be a Prophecy written by the Prophet Eddie Vedder from one of my favorite bands Pearl Jam.

Photo: On August 10th, 2021 this incredible angel sylph wing appeared directly above Phoenix, Arizona after working with retinal surgeons in surgery to restore vision.

Photo: On August 10th, 2021 this incredible pair of angel's sylph faces appeared in central Arizona.

Photo: On August 10th, 2021 this incredible angel sylph wing appeared directly above our home in Prescott Valley, Arizona.

Photo: On August 10th, 2021 this incredible angel sylph wing appeared directly above our home in Prescott Valley, Arizona.

Photo: On August 10th, 2021 this incredible angel sylph wing sunset appeared directly above our home in Prescott Valley, Arizona.

Photo: On August 10th, 2021 this incredible angel sylph wing appeared directly above our home in Prescott Valley, Arizona.

Photo: On August 10th, 2021 this incredibly mysterious angel sylph winged sunset appeared directly above our home in Prescott Valley, Arizona.

CHAPTER TWO:
"Venus Trine Mars"

The Lion's Gate Portal opening brought about the "sacred dance" of Venus and Mars. When we see what is called the Venus trine Mars — with Venus and Mars in Aquarius — these energies are magnified.

The next parade of angelic sightings is among the most powerfully magnificent I've ever seen. Not only did I start to personally witness the "dancing" of Venus in the night sky, including shimmering and turning different colors, but I also have video recordings of every star in the Orion Nebula doing the same (remember my hypothesis of the human race being descendants of a race of alien Anunnaki from the Orion Nebula).

All these events are precursors to what I believe is the return of our True King, whose identity has been revealed in my previous books. In astrology, each year, our sun, the earth, and Sirius align with the pyramids of Giza (you will see multiple "pyramid" shaped clouds in the photos) to open a special window of intense energy that changes how we look at ourselves and the world.

Since this is an "11" year in astrology, the focus is on new soul-rich relationships and working on soul contracts that we came to earth from Orion to fulfill. One particularly interesting event is that many of the angel photos were taken right around "11:11a.m."

Our soul contracts focus on unconditional love, forgiveness, patience, and acceptance. It is no wonder that in my previous book "Kingdom Come", I witnessed the "infinity" symbol in the skies I photographed after asking for this sign from Mother Mary. "11:11" is a sign of awakening and ascension, and it also closely correlates to twin flames and soul relationships.

Photo: Annunaki Angels appearing after the Lion's Gate portal opening in August of 2021. These are very powerful angels meant to help us during trying times on earth.

Photo: more Anunnaki Angels appearing after the Lion's Gate portal opening in August of 2021. These are very powerful angels meant to help us during trying times on earth.

Photo: more Anunnaki Angels appearing after the Lion's Gate portal opening in August of 2021. These are very powerful angels meant to help us during trying times on earth.

Photo: more Anunnaki Angels appearing after the Lion's Gate portal opening in August of 2021. These are very powerful angels meant to help us during trying times on earth. You can see how their presence dramatically affects our sunrises and sunsets.

Photo: more Anunnaki Angels appearing after the Lion's Gate portal opening in August of 2021. These are very powerful angels meant to help us during trying times on earth.

Photo: more Anunnaki Angels appearing after the Lion's Gate portal opening in August of 2021. These are very powerful angels meant to help us during trying times on earth.

Photo: more Anunnaki Angels appearing after the Lion's Gate portal opening in August of 2021. These are very powerful angels meant to help us during trying times on earth. You can see to the top left one of them is forming an Anunnaki "pyramid."

Photo: more Anunnaki Angels appearing after the Lion's Gate portal opening in August of 2021. These are very powerful angels meant to help us during trying times on earth. Take special notice of the huge sunlit wing in the top middle and the huge angel cloud wing bottom middle.

Photo: more Anunnaki Angels appearing after the Lion's Gate portal opening in August of 2021. These are very powerful angels meant to help us during trying times on earth.

Photo: more Anunnaki Angels appearing after the Lion's Gate portal opening in August of 2021. These are very powerful angels meant to help us during trying times on earth.

Photo: more Anunnaki Angels appearing after the Lion's Gate portal opening in August of 2021. These are very powerful angels meant to help us during trying times on earth. Look at the huge face to the left in the middle row.

Photo: more Anunnaki Angels appearing after the Lion's Gate portal opening in August of 2021. These are very powerful angels meant to help us during trying times on earth. Take note of the face in the middle of the bottom row and a sunlit cross on its left cheek.

Photo: more Annunaki Angels appearing after the Lion's Gate portal opening in August of 2021. These are very powerful angels meant to help us during trying times on earth. Some of these colors are absolutely royal and glorious.

Photo: more Annunaki Angels appearing after the Lion's Gate portal opening in August of 2021. These are very powerful angels meant to help us during trying times on earth. Look at some of these huge winged messengers of God (Anunnaki Adonai).

Photo: more Annunaki Angels appearing after the Lion's Gate portal opening in August of 2021. These are very powerful angels meant to help us during trying times on earth. Some of these images of these wings are breathtaking.

Photo: more Anunnaki Angels appearing after the Lion's Gate portal opening in August of 2021. These are very powerful angels meant to help us during trying times on earth. They are here to try to steer this world towards peace in all things.

Photo: more Annunaki Angels appearing after the Lion's Gate portal opening in August of 2021. These are very powerful angels meant to help us during trying times on earth. Look at the face in the top middle row.

Photo: more Anunnaki Angels appearing after the Lion's Gate portal opening in August of 2021. These are very powerful angels meant to help us during trying times on earth. These were taken at some close friends who visited me from Michigan my home state. Look at the huge angel head far left middle row.

Photo: more Annunaki Angels appearing after the Lion's Gate portal opening in August of 2021. These are very powerful angels meant to help us during trying times on earth. These were taken by some close friends who visited me from Michigan my home state.

Photo: more Anunnaki Angels appearing after the Lion's Gate portal opening in August of 2021. These are very powerful angels meant to help us during trying times on earth. These were taken at some close friends who visited me from Michigan my home state. Look at some of these sunlit angel wings.

Photo: more Annunaki Angels appearing after the Lion's Gate portal opening in August of 2021. These are very powerful angels meant to help us during trying times on earth. Look at the huge angel in flight in the left and middle frames of the top row and the one bottom right. Simply powerful and amazing.

Photo: more Annunaki Angels appearing after the Lion's Gate portal opening in August of 2021. These are very powerful angels meant to help us during trying times on earth. Some of these angel wings cover the entire sky.

Photo: more Annunaki Angels appearing after the Lion's Gate portal opening in August of 2021. These are very powerful angels meant to help us during trying times on earth. Look at the radiance of the sunsets and sunrises here in the Fall of 2021. Do you see the fallen angel being exorcised in the top right frame?

Photo: more Annunaki Angels appearing after the Lion's Gate portal opening in August of 2021. These are very powerful angels meant to help us during trying times on earth. Do you see the cross in the left middle row?

Photo: more Anunnaki Angels appearing after the Lion's Gate portal opening in August of 2021. These are very powerful angels meant to help us during trying times on earth. Do you see the feathered wing within the huge wing in the middle row to the far left?

Photo: more Anunnaki Angels appearing after the Lion's Gate portal opening in August of 2021. These are very powerful angels meant to help us during trying times on earth. Do you see the pyramid shape in the middle photo of the middle row?

Photo: more Anunnaki Angels appearing after the Lion's Gate portal opening in August of 2021. These are very powerful angels meant to help us during trying times on earth. Do you see the angel forming a cross in the far-left frame of the middle row?

Photo: more Anunnaki Angels appearing after the Lion's Gate portal opening in August of 2021. These are very powerful angels meant to help us during trying times on earth. If you look closely, you can see Mother Mary's face in the far-left frame in the bottom row.

Photo: more Annunaki Angels appearing after the Lion's Gate portal opening in August of 2021. These are very powerful angels meant to help us during trying times on earth. Do you see yet another pyramid shaped angel in the middle row to the far right?

Photo: more Anunnaki Angels appearing after the Lion's Gate portal opening in August of 2021. These are very powerful angels meant to help us during trying times on earth.

Photo: more Anunnaki Angels appearing after the Lion's Gate portal opening in August of 2021. These are very powerful angels meant to help us during trying times on earth.

Photo: more Anunnaki Angels appearing after the Lion's Gate portal opening in August of 2021. These are very powerful angels meant to help us during trying times on earth. I see another horse head of the apocalypse in the top middle frame.

Photo: more Anunnaki Angels appearing after the Lion's Gate portal opening in August of 2021. These are very powerful angels meant to help us during trying times on earth. The letters H, Z, M, and G can be seen here in honor of some angels whose name starts with those letters that I've helped loved ones connect with.

Photo: more Annunaki Angels appearing after the Lion's Gate portal opening in August of 2021. These are very powerful angels meant to help us during trying times on earth. Do you see another pyramid in the top right frame? I like to call the angel to the far right in the middle row the "Elvis Angel" because he looks like Elvis to me.

Photo: more Anunnaki Angels appearing after the Lion's Gate portal opening in August of 2021. These are very powerful angels meant to help us during trying times on earth. There are some remarkable moonlit angels here in the bottom row as well as a blue heart and pyramid on fire sunset.

Photo: more Anunnaki Angels appearing after the Lion's Gate portal opening in August of 2021. These are very powerful angels meant to help us during trying times on earth. Look at the phoenix looking winged angel in the middle frame middle row.

Photo: more Anunnaki Angels appearing after the Lion's Gate portal opening in August of 2021. These are very powerful angels meant to help us during trying times on earth. The huge face in the middle frame middle row is unmistakably angel.

CHAPTER THREE:
G is for Greg

As I progress through this journey, many encounters have had a profound impact on my life. But very few times have I been truly amazed by the power of the other kingdom.

Certainly, Paxton's story from The New Wine and The Veil Rent is one exception. I encountered a lovely lady named Megan Montieth. She had read a post on Facebook about my ability to contact lost loved ones. Megan sent me a private message with a photo of her husband Greg Montieth, who suddenly passed away in November 2021 after a bout with COVID.

Megan was happy to receive anything I could get from Greg that he was doing okay in his next life. After a Rosary at a local church for Greg and Megan, I received the following images: a bicycle, a stuffed teddy bear, a tea kettle, and a plant. After relaying this information to Megan, she was amazed, stating they had bought their daughter Emma a bike for her birthday the year before, and she and Greg would walk behind her as she rode the bike, and she had bought her son a stuffed grief bear because he was missing his father. Megan also mentioned that she was given a tea set and a plant after Greg's passing.

After informing Megan that I asked St. Mary and our Angels to show us a huge G in the skies for Greg, knowing that our prayers had been answered and that Greg was truly with the angels now. Megan stated she believes he is aware of everything that has happened in his family since his passing, and that he has watched the outpouring of love and support from family, friends, neighbors, and strangers since Greg's death.

After looking at my photos from the days before and after Greg's death, I began to suspect something else. I began to believe Greg was likely one of our Anunnaki Angel half-breeds, essentially an earth angel from heaven. The following photos show from the day before Greg's death, the day of his death, and the day after his death lead me to believe he was a high order incarnate angel. Within days of Megan and I's initial contact and my prayers for Greg, we were both able to photograph over 30 large "G's" in the skies. From the response, we have no doubt been sent from the other kingdom by a new angel named Greg.

Photo: Greg and Megan Montieth with their three lovely children while visiting Stonehenge.

Photo: The incredibly angelic skies blowing up the day prior to Greg Montieth's untimely passing and the day of and following his death. Some of the angels shown here are some of the bests I've ever seen and the sunsets and sunrises are beyond compare. It is no doubt these angels were coming to this earth to retrieve one of their own. You can also see some fallen angel faces in these photos being exorcised from the earth by the more powerful angels and angel Greg.

Photo: More than thirty large "G's" were photographed in multiple states by myself and Megan Montieth sent by our angels from the other kingdom in honor of Greg Montieth who lost his battle with COVID in November of 2021. See the "G" on the angel's chest?

CHAPTER FOUR:
A Shower of Roses

The next story is one of the most amazing experiences I've ever had. I was recently in St. George, Utah working with local retinal surgeons when I visited St. George Catholic Church. If you read my book "The Precious Blood", this is where the precious blood miracle occurred. My friend told me that the Vatican actually has the blood tested in a laboratory.

In any event, after Mass, I encountered a woman named Diane. For some reason, I felt compelled to show her one of my angel photos, and we got to talking about my books. Diane was sweet and asked if I would pray with her in front of a statue of St. Theresa in the Church.

As we stood in front of a statue of St. Theresa and said some Hail Mary's, I asked for Diane to be healed. She had been injured in a car accident in her teens. I asked Diane what she would like to see later in the skies. Diane said without hesitation, "a rose."

What happened in the skies above St. George, Utah was simply amazing? A dozen roses appeared in the skies. A few days later, I received a text from my friend stating that a prayer card to

St. Theresa was inexplicably found in the church that morning; titled, "a shower of roses."

In one photo of the rose, you can see a small dog's face. Diane owns, he dies almost a week earlier.

Photo: This was the first "rose" we received above St. George, Utah in early January 2022 after praying with a new friend named Diane. The amazing thing about this photo is you can see a small dog's face right below the sun. Diane had recently almost lost a dog whose face looked just like this "angel dog."

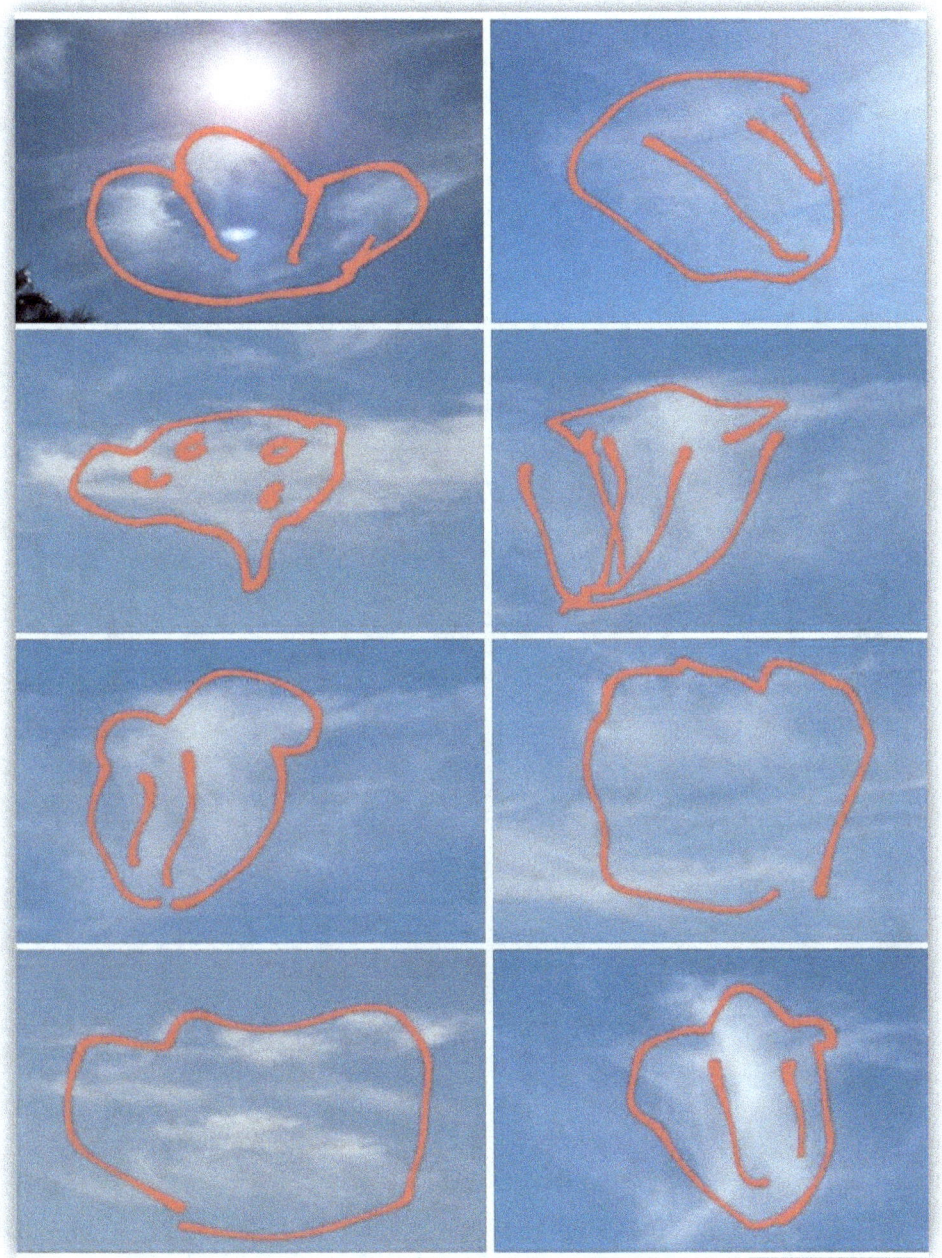

Photo: These beautiful roses appeared above St. George, Utah in early 2022 after praying with a new friend named Diane for healing and for a sign our prayers were heard.

Photo: An incredible photo of more roses, a huge "D" in the skies, and the "shower of roses" prayer card to St. Theresa found in the church soon after I prayed with a new friend named Diane.

Photo: These incredible angles appeared directly above St. George, Utah after we received a dozen roses following prayers with a new friend named Diane who had asked to see a rose in the skies.

Photo: These incredible angles appeared directly above St. George, Utah after we received a dozen roses following prayers with a new friend named Diane who had asked to see a rose in the skies.

Photo: These incredible angles appeared directly above St. George, Utah after we received a dozen roses following prayers with a new friend named Diane who had asked to see a rose in the skies.

Photo: These incredible angles appeared directly above St. George, Utah after we received a dozen roses following prayers with a new friend named Diane who had asked to see a rose in the skies.

CHAPTER FIVE:
J is for Jeff

It is with a heavy heart that I write this next chapter. On January 16th, 2022, the world lost an incredible incarnate angel named Jeff Cadieux. Jeff is my wife's first cousin, Carol Rose. He was a year younger than me.

I recall many Christmas dinners with him at his mom Dale and Dad Mike's home in Chesterfield, Michigan. Needless to say, both Carol and I were heartbroken; we are still in shock.

Everyone who knew Jeff witnessed firsthand his humor and generosity towards others. Jeff and his lovely wife Amy have three beautiful children, Emma, David, and David Angelus.

In my experience with so many afterlife connections for other families, I knew the steps to show his family he is still with us. However, I found the process painful, it made the situation too real.

In any event, the morning of Jeff's funeral services in Macomb, Michigan, my wife (who is spiritually powerful) and I entered a Catholic Church in Macomb, and as we touched hands next to a statue of St. Mary, we said three Hail Mary's and asked St. Mary to send us a huge "J" in the skies as a sign Jeff is now with the angels.

The outpouring of hope brought us to tears. I was simply amazed throughout the day. I photographed over twenty "J's" in the skies directly above the funeral home. One of the photos even has a "V" next to a "J", which I took as meaning Jeff is now victorious and has a new life in Christ.

Photo: The memory card from the obituary for our dearly departed cousin Jeff Cadieux.

Photo: A recent photo of Jeffrey Cadieux and his beautiful bride Amy.

Photo: All of these incredible angels appeared shortly after Jeff's untimely passing in January of 2022. You can clearly see the first two "J's" we received from St. Mary and the angels in honor of Jeff's new life with them. In one photo here you can actually see a young man with long hair and a small dog face beneath him. Jeff had long hair when he was young.

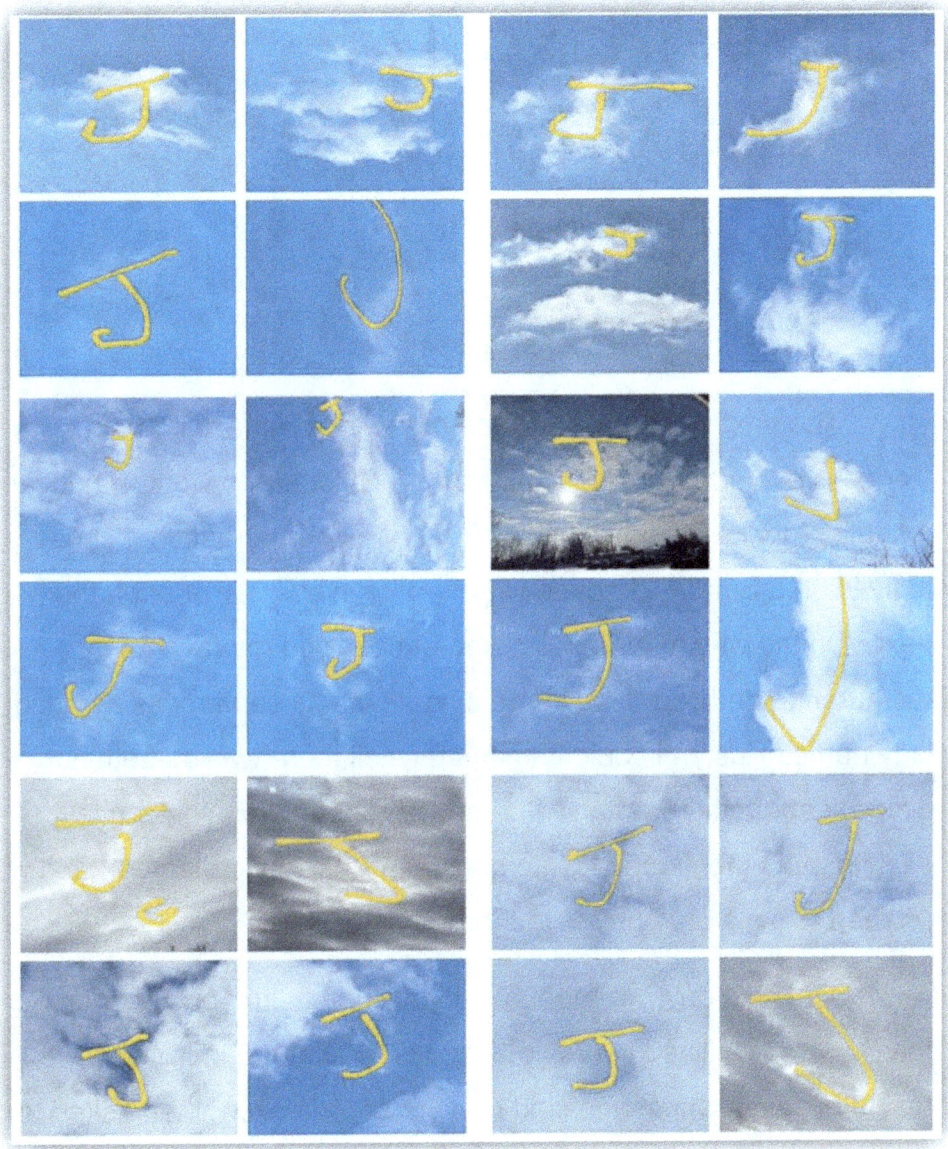

Photo: An incredible display of angel power from the other kingdom of heaven as twenty-four huge "J's" appeared in the skies above the funeral home in Macomb, Michigan as we celebrated the life of an amazing earth angel Jeffrey Cadieux.

CHAPTER SIX:
K is for Kristy

The next story is simply one of the most amazing angel stories I've ever had. I was in Durango, Colorado to work with local retinal surgeons in mid-February 2022. For some reason, I chose to fly in on a Sunday, because I had to be in surgery at noon the next. On the way to dinner, instead of choosing my favorite restaurant, I decided to try something new. My server was a young lady named Kristy. I could immediately tell there was something different about this woman. She had an energy I couldn't quite explain, but I mentioned I write books on Angels. She agreed and listened to my story on how to summon them.

The next day, we meet at a local church, so I could teach her the prayers I've listed in previous books. We stood in front of a statue of Jesus Christ and said prayers of protection, then asked to see Arch Angels in the skies and a giant "K" for Kristy. I was simply astounded by what happened over the next two days in Durango. We witnessed Venus's shimmering, changing colors the night after we said prayers at the local church. All of which was caught on video. The photos in this chapter show my feelings for Kristy being one of our half-breed Anunnaki Angels, which was confirmed.

The other amazing portion of Kristy's story was that the morning I met her, she wrote on her bathroom mirror, "I will have a magical life."

Kristy mentioned she was told her daughter was a 'crystal child' at the time of her birth. Amazingly enough, her daughter could clairvoyantly see that I had given Kristy a "crystal" Rosary. I picked it up the day before my trip, unknowing the reason. I just thought it was beautiful.

Photo: The morning after meeting and praying with a new half breed angel named Kristy this angelic sunrise appeared above Durango, Colorado in mid-February 2022.

Photo: Three huge "K's" appear after meeting and praying with a new angel named "Kristy" above Durango, Colorado.

Photo: More angels appear above Colorado in mid-February after meeting and praying with an angel named Kristy.

Photo: More "K's" appear in the skies above Durango, Colorado in mid-February 2022 after meeting and praying with a new angel named Kristy.

Photo: Huge angels appear above Colorado in mid-February after meeting and praying with an angel named Kristy.

Photo: An incredible sighting of Venus and amazing angelic sunset above Durango, Colorado in mid-February 2022 after meeting and praying with an angel named Kristy.

Photo: Huge angels appear above Durango, Colorado in mid-February 2022 after meeting and praying with an angel named Kristy.

Photo: Incredibly huge Arch Angels appear in the skies above Durango, Colorado in mid-February 2022 after meeting and praying with an angel named Kristy.

CHAPTER SEVEN:
The Qui Tam Case and A Canary

In 2021, an article in the headlines read "Bausch Health defeats drug reps retaliation claims." I was the "drug rep" mentioned in the article.

The case was lost; from 2014 to 2017, I worked as a pharmaceutical sales representative in the Midwest, promoting a new "fifth-generation" antibiotic to local eye surgeons and optometrists in the area. As reps, we were all also tasked with promoting a new supposedly more convenient online pharmacy program named "Philidor." The supposed advantage of this new online pharmacy was to deliver drugs to a patient's house by the next day.

The company told us to promote this program, which also offered the patient a rebate to our doctors. About midway through this promotion, the Federal Government brought criminal charges against two of our company executives for running an illegal kickback scheme. As it turns out, the two conspired to steal more than $50 million of the profits from these filled prescriptions.

After questioning upper management in a meeting, simply asking "how do you want me to address this in my offices?" My services were no longer needed, and I was fired.

My attorney believed the case fell into a strong, "Qui Tam" situation, which protects corporate "whistleblowers" from illegal termination of employment for reporting criminal activity (I had also reported to the FDA illegal off-label promotion that was part of this scam).

If I have one pet peeve, it's greed...., especially greed targeted at the elderly and lower-income populations. The point of all this is to describe what happened after we filed this justified lawsuit, in which any monies were recovered. I planned on paying most of it (after paying my attorney) to the victims of this scam.

Needless to say, on the same day, the Arizona Federal Judge decided unjustly to throw our case out, largely due to missing a filing deadline. Plus, the case was his word against hers, the Cumbre Vieja volcano in the La Palma in the Canary Islands erupted. It spewed lava for 85 straight days.

Now I know what you are thinking, "this guy isn't suggesting the judges' unjust ruling was the cause of the volcano eruption in the Canary Islands, is he?"

I admit it would be an interesting coincidence, but a coincidence nonetheless, if it were not for this simple fact.

The eruption not only occurred on the same day the judge made his decision but also in the Canary Islands. A "whistleblower" is also referred to by many as a "canary."

The damage estimates are over 843 billion dollars. What's also interesting is the image of one house miraculously saved from the volcanic fires. The press referred to this house as "the miracle of La Palma." I am willing to bet there was a crucifix in that home or, at least, a statue of St. Mary.

Photo: The Cumbre Vieja volcano erupts on September 19th, 2022 in the Canary Islands off the coast of Spain.

Photo: The "miracle house" of the Cumbre Vieja volcanic eruptions that were miraculously spared of surrounding fires from the volcano.

Photo: An interesting looking cross formed from lava erupting from the Cumbre Vieja volcano in the Canary Islands near Spain in the fall of 2021.

Photo: An aerial view of the Cumbre Vieja volcano in the Canary Islands near Spain in the fall of 2021.

CHAPTER EIGHT:
Apocalypse Now

As I wrote in The Precious Blood; Matthew 24:6-14 warns of wars and rumors of wars, kingdom rising up against kingdom, earthquakes, pestilence, and famines in diverse places seems to certainly fit the current state of affairs in early 2022.

Some apocalyptic events have definitely happened since the start of 2021. Consider the volcanic eruptions that occurred over fifty times from Mt. Etna in Italy. The Iceland volcanic eruptions, not to mention the massive eruptions from Kilauea in Hawaii. Plus, the La Cumbre Vieja volcano in the Canary Islands erupted for over eighty-five days, and the volcano in Congo erupted, sending thousands fleeing.

In July, researchers discovered the remains of an underwater volcano named the "Eye of Sauron" and it is a clear reference to Satan in my opinion. In August, three Alaskan volcanoes erupted simultaneously. The eruption near Tonga, which created a tsunami, was more powerful than a nuclear bomb and equaled ten megatons of force, as scientists said it "rang the atmosphere" like a bell while destroying an entire island. We also witnessed the first recorded tsunami that hit every ocean. Plus, a four hundred- and seventy-seven-mile-long lighting strike.

The earthquakes range from 4.0 to 8.0 magnitude, including massive wildfires, and deadly flooding. 2021 was the third most active hurricane season on record, with twenty-one named storms that caused $80 billion in damage.

As we observe Russia 2022 massing at the border of Ukraine threatening a possible major military invasion, we also see North Korea testing long-term missiles that could hit the United States, as both Russia and China continue to test new hypersonic weapons.

In early 2022, we saw a major cyclone named Batsirai leaving many homeless and killing over ninety-two. Including major variants of the COVID virus, which may have been "weaponized" in China. This pandemic has been used to trample human rights, especially among healthcare workers, many of whom have lost their jobs for refusing a vaccine.

As witnessed by millions, we seem to be living the book of Revelations; with one question, yet left unanswered. Is the Devil winning?

Photo: I took this photo in early August 2021 and it appears to be a huge hand giving the middle finger. It would be funny to me if it were not how all of 2021 felt to many of us. Is this what our God thinks of this world? Wouldn't he be justified if so?

Photo: As I wrote about in the book The Precious Blood many believe the Denver International Airport to be run by "alien reptilian lizard people" that inhabit our Elites and plan to hide underground following an Apocalypse. This sign appears to either be making fun of the "conspiracy theories" or flat outputting the truth in plain sight under our noses.

Photo: Another mural mocking the idea that alien reptilian lizard people are building underground bunkers beneath the Denver International Airport. Is this just a "conspiracy theory"?

Photo: Apocalyptic looking wildfires scorch Northern California in early 2022.

Photo: The Wolf volcano in Ecuador erupted in early 2022 producing the river of fire and giving us another apocalyptic image.

Photo: The massive and violent eruption of the volcano near Tonga rang the atmosphere like a bell and produced this lighting storm in a major apocalyptic event in December of 2021 that lasted for four weeks.

Photo: A nearly four hundred- and seventy-seven-mile bolt of lightning strikes along the Gulf Coast in 2020 set a record.

CHAPTER NINE:
Twin Queens

In my previous publications, I mentioned that I believe in parallel dimensions, and humans are creations of a race known as Anunnaki from the Orion Nebula.

Anunnaki literally means "from the heavens or skies."

The defining marker of this race is the elongated skull. Remains from archaeological digs have been found. On 02-21-22, a perfect numerical palindrome, I was fortunate enough to photograph twin Anunnaki Queens in the skies above my home in Prescott Valley, Arizona.

One of these twin queens actually holds what appears to be a baby angel. What is truly remarkable about these appearances is of all the angel sightings I had leading up to this day started on Friday, February 18th, 2022, and continued until the morning of February 22nd, 2022. It should also be noted that the date of 022222 is also considered significant, especially as we continue to see hints in our skies that the Anunnaki may return to earth soon.

It must also be noted that in 022122, as Vladimir Putin decided to invade Ukraine against the world's wishes, Mt. Etna exploded in a spectacular display of the power of Mother Nature on earth.

Anunnaki Queen. Recent archaeological digs have unearthed such skulls. Many believe the ancient Anunnaki not only built our pyramids but seeded the human race and will return one day soon. Recent signs I have documented support this theory as does the show Ancient Aliens.

Photo: An incredible photo of an Anunnaki Queen Angel holding a baby angel was taken near my home in central Arizona on 022122 which is a perfect numerical palindrome suggesting "two become one."

Photo: A second Anunnaki Queen angel in the skies with the elongated cranium arms outstretched as photographed on 022122 a perfect numerical palindrome above my home in central Arizona.

Photo: These incredible signs and wonders were photographed in the days leading up to the twin Queen Anunnaki angel sightings beginning on February 18th, 2022. You can clearly see wings in these images and a moon visible to the naked eye during the day.

Photo: Incredible images of angels appearing above central Arizona during a morning Mass for world peace on Sunday, February 20th, 2022 a date with all numerical 2s and 0s.

Photo: Incredible images of angels appearing above central Arizona during a morning Mass for world peace on Sunday, February 20th, 2022 a date with all numerical 2s and 0s.

Photo: Incredible images of angels appearing above central Arizona during a morning Mass for world peace on Sunday, February 20th, 2022 a date with all numerical 2s and 0s. There are numerous "Zs" and pyramid shapes in the images along with huge faces and clear angels in flight.

Photo: Incredible images of angels appearing above central Arizona during a morning Mass for world peace on Sunday, February 20th, 2022 a date with all numerical 2s and 0s. The angel in flight top left is one of the best angel photos I have ever taken.

Photo: Incredible images of angels appearing above central Arizona during a morning Mass for world peace on Sunday, February 20th, 2022 a date with all numerical 2s and 0s.

Photo: Incredible images of angels appearing above central Arizona during a morning Mass for world peace on Sunday, February 21st, 2022 a date that is a perfect numerical palindrome. The second Anunnaki Queen angel can be seen on the bottom right frame.

Photo: An incredible image of the sunset the evening of February 20th, 2022 shows three suns as orbs, and a huge angel face. The bottom row shows the first Anunnaki Queen angel holding a baby on 022122 a numerical palindrome.

Photo: Incredible images of angels, a huge cross, and a family of angels next to a pyramid at sunset as well as the second Anunnaki Queen angel all appeared on 022122 a perfect numerical palindrome date. The sunset is clearly a glimpse of Heaven/Eden/An.

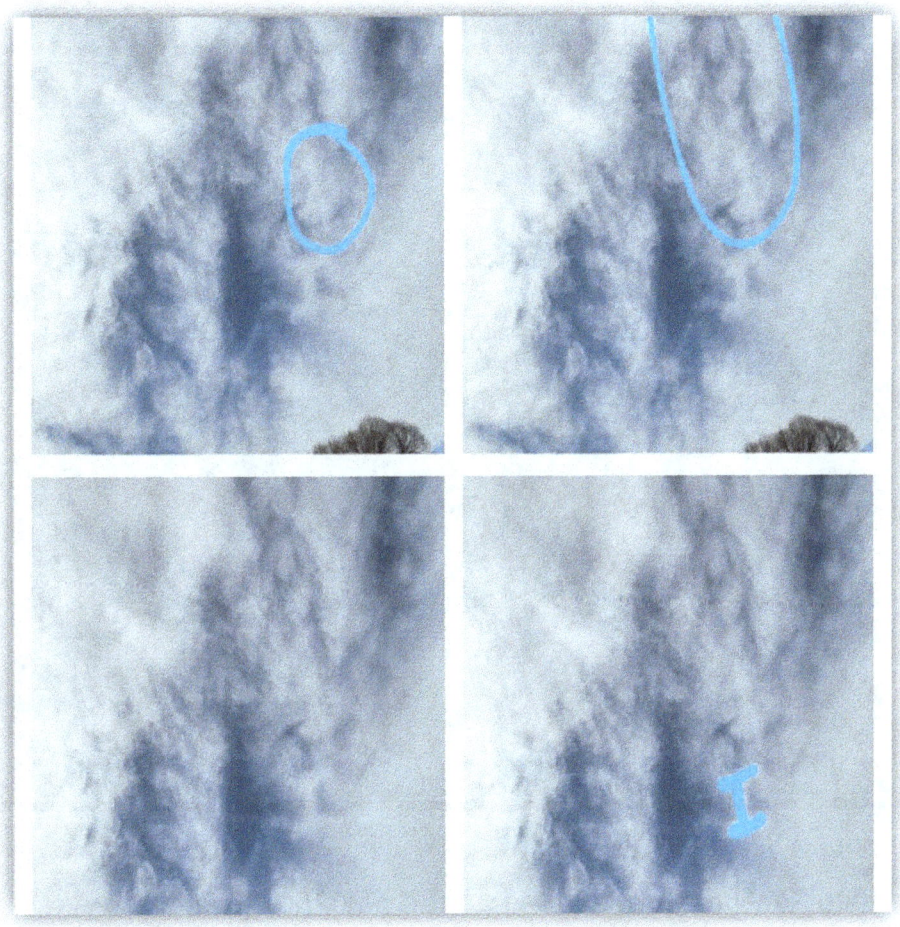

Photo: Another incredible event occurred on 022122 as this angelic figure appeared seemingly holding out its hand as a large capital "I" can be seen below a smaller infantile angel figure. The significance of the "I" could mean the human race as the "Ido" or offspring of the Anunnaki who are here to enforce world peace amongst its seeded race.

Photo: An incredible event occurred on 02/21/22 at dusk. After witnessing one of the most amazing sunsets, I've even seen in addition to seeing twin Anunnaki Queen angels and a pyramid at sunset next to an angel family my wife called me to our back porch where these two intertwined feathers were found next to our home. I saw no birds near our property that day at all.

Photo: On 02/21/22 as Russian Premier Vladimir Putin decided to invade the Ukraine Mt. Etna exploded in a violent eruption blanketing the entire sky.

CHAPTER TEN:
Addendum

I want to share something miraculously amazing that occurred the same day I submitted this manuscript to my literary agent on Valentine's Day, February 14th, 2022. I went out to look at the sunset, which is a daily routine. As I got to my normal parking space in my neighborhood, I took out my cell phone to get a few pictures. In the gallery, I found an incredible photograph I did not take.

The miraculous thing about the image was my cell phone lens was covered, resting on the console in the car. A song on the radio was playing, 'Blinded by the Light' later followed by 'Angel of the Morning.'

There is no scientific or logical explanation for this photo, but something profound is happening to my face. As incredible as this "accidental" photograph, I also received a handwritten letter in the mail just after submitting my new book on angels and heaven to my literary agent. In light of this message, we can be assured, God's promise will be upheld.

Photo: An unexplained photograph of my face covered in total light. You can see my shirt which is what I was wearing at the time. My cell phone was completely covered when this occurred after submitting my next book on Angels on Valentine's Day February 14th, 2022.

Photo: The incredible views of huge angels and more pyramids and a very radiant sunset with a pyramid appeared in central Arizona on Valentine's Day, February 14th, 2022 as I submitted this new book to my literary agent for publication.

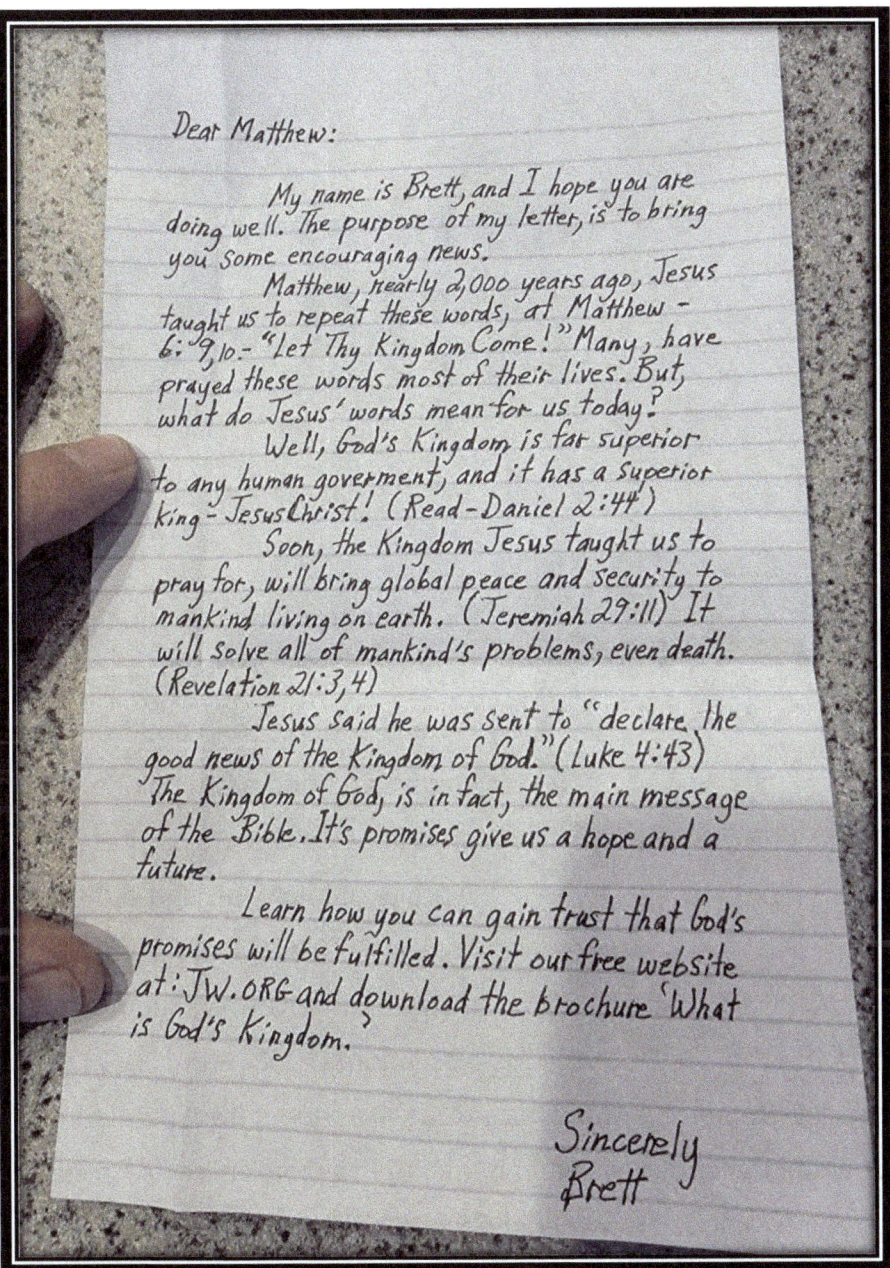

Photo: This incredible letter speaking of the Kingdom of Heaven and quotes from Matthew appeared in my mailbox the same day I finished my seventh book on angels and heaven

About the Author

Matthew Douglas Pinard is the author of The New Wine series. He was born and raised in southeastern Michigan and has a bachelor's degree in psychology from the University of Michigan and a master's degree in military history from Louisiana State University. Matthew is also a former US Army JAG legal specialist. He and his wife Carol Rose are recent transplants from west Michigan and now live in beautiful Prescott Valley, Arizona, with their two dogs Reese, a chocolate Lab, and Cleetus, a Redbone Coonhound. Matthew is a ranked Shihan (sixth degree) in Hakko Den shin Ryu Japanese Jujutsu and enjoys hiking, communing with the other side, praying for world peace, and photographing archangels in his spare time.

OTHER BOOKS BY AUTHOR MATTHEW

matthewpinardauthor.com

Follow Me:

- [Goodreads](#)
- [Author Central](#)
- [YouTube](#)

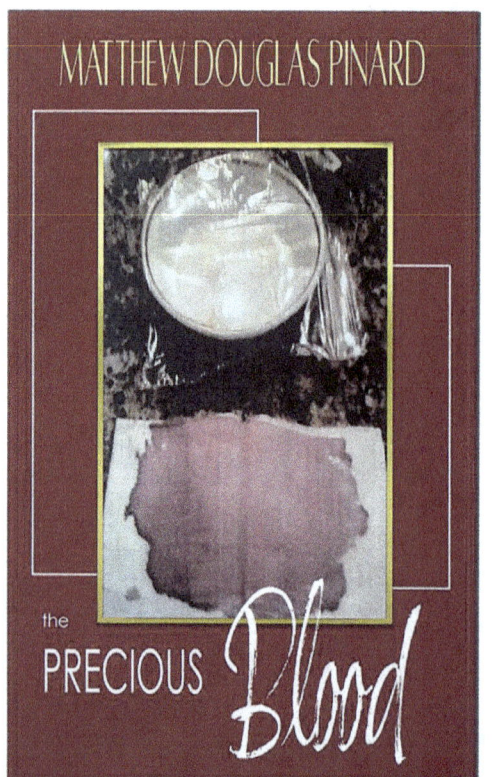

MATTHEW DOUGLAS PINARD

@matthewpinardauthor.com

SCREENPLAY AWARDS
MATTHEW DOUGLAS

Official Selection

Bloodstained Indie Film Festival

StoryPros Awards Screenplay Contest

Military Script Showcase

L.A. Neo Noir Novel Film & Script Festival

True Story International Film Festival

Reel Heart International Film Festival

Hollywood Boulevard International Film Festival

Independent Talents International Film Festival

Fort Worth Indie Film Showcase

California Independent Film Festival

San Pedro International Film Festival,

Southeastern International Film Festival

Louisiana International Film Festival

Official Selection

First Ten Pages Script Contest

Atlanta Comedy Film Festival

Georgia Shorts Film Festival

Official Finalist

[Las Vegas International Film and Screenwriting Contest](#), Honorable Mention

[Depth of Field International Film Festival](#), Award Winner

[Beverly Hills International Film Festival](#), Silver Winner

[Queen Palm International Film Festival](#), Award Winner

[Colorado International Film Festival](#), Quarter-Finalist

[Chicago Screenplay Awards](#), Quarter-Finalist

[NYC International Screenplay Awards](#), Quarter-Finalist

[Atlanta Screenplay Awards](#), Semi-Finalist

[Cordillera International Film Festival](#), Semi-Finalist

[Fade In Awards](#), Finalist

[Breaking Walls Thriller Screenplay](#) Award Winner

[Vegas Movie Awards](#),

[The Santa Barbara International Screenplay Awards](#), Finalist

[Miami Screen Play Awards,](#) Quarter-Finalist:

www.ingramcontent.com/pod-product-compliance
Lightning Source LLC
Chambersburg PA
CBHW081359070526
44583CB00020B/2596